THE ANCIENT WORLD

ANCIENT EGYPT

BY NEL YOMTOV

CHILDREN'S PRESS®
AN IMPRINT OF SCHOLASTIC INC.
NEW YORK TORONTO LONDON AUCKLAND SYDNEY
MEXICO CITY NEW DELHI HONG KONG
DANBURY, CONNECTICUT

Content Consultant
Willeke Wendrich, PhD
Professor of Egyptian Archaeology/Digital Humanities
University of California, Los Angeles

Library of Congress Cataloging-in-Publication Data
Yomtov, Nelson.
  Ancient Egypt/by Nel Yomtov.
    p. cm.—(The ancient world)
  Includes bibliographical references and index.
  ISBN: 978-0-531-25177-5 (lib. bdg.)   ISBN: 978-0-531-25977-1 (pbk.)
1. Egypt—History—Juvenile literature. 2. Egypt—Civilization—To 332 B.C.—Juvenile literature. I. Title.
  DT60.Y66 2012
  932—dc23   2012001246

Maps by XNR Productions, Inc.

1 2 3 4 5 6 7 8 9 10 R 22 21 20 19 18 17 16 15 14 13

More than 5,000 years ago, ancient Egypt first began to develop along the banks of the Nile River.

At the time of Ramses III temples owned about one-third of all the farmable land in Egypt.

Cleopatra's death ended the 3,200-year reign of the Egyptian pharaohs.

JOURNEY BACK TO ANCIENT EGYPT

TABLE OF CONTENTS

*Senwosret I wearing the
white crown of Upper Egypt*

Burial mask of Tutankhamen

The Past Is Present
See for yourself how ancient Egypt is still present in our lives today.

THE GIFT OF THE NILE

To modern people ancient Egypt may appear to be distant and difficult to understand. After all, Egyptian civilization began more than five thousand years ago, in the darkness of prehistory. But from its incredible architecture—pyramids,

The Temple of Ramses II is one of the many examples of the ancient Egyptians' incredible architectural abilities.

temples, and monuments—to the exquisite works of art and the gold and precious stones used to decorate priceless objects, ancient Egypt has left behind a remarkable legacy.

The passage of time has not dimmed our interest in this grand civilization along the Nile River. Four thousand years have passed since the colossal Great Pyramid at Giza was built. Two thousand years have elapsed since the reign of the last Egyptian **pharaoh**. In the time since these events, however, important elements of Egyptian culture have vanished. Ancient Egyptian religion has disappeared, giving way to Christianity and then to Islam. **Hieroglyphs**, the symbols with which the ancient Egyptian

Many of the ancient Egyptians' most impressive works of art were found inside tombs.

pharaoh (FAIR-oh) ancient Egyptian ruler

hieroglyphs (HYE-roh-glifs) ancient Egyptian writing system made up of pictures and symbols

language was written, vanished from use—and remained indecipherable by later cultures until a remarkable eighteenth-century archaeological find, the Rosetta Stone.

Ancient Egypt amassed an amazing list of accomplishments. In architecture and engineering, structures such as the Great Pyramid and the Temple of Karnak have never been equaled in size or accuracy of construction. In medicine, the ancient Egyptians were unsurpassed until the later decades of the Greek Empire. In government, Egyptian leadership was stable, and ruled and served its subjects throughout Egypt's three thousand-year history. The Egyptians were also pioneers in mathematics, astronomy, art, and technology. Equally important, they spread their knowledge to nearby cultures, which in turn spread them throughout the ancient world.

One important key to unlocking the mysteries of ancient Egypt has been the Egyptians' passion for writing and for creating paintings in the burial places of their dead. The Egyptians were among the first people to develop writing and inks. Using hieroglyphs, they wrote on **papyrus** scrolls, on temple walls and columns, and in books. They made lists of their property, described battles, and told tales of their gods. The Egyptians decorated the tombs of their mighty pharaohs with paintings depicting the

The Rosetta Stone is on display to the public at the British Museum in London, England.

papyrus (puh-PYE-ruhss) paper made from the stems of the papyrus plant, a tall water plant that grows in northern Africa

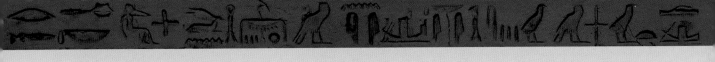

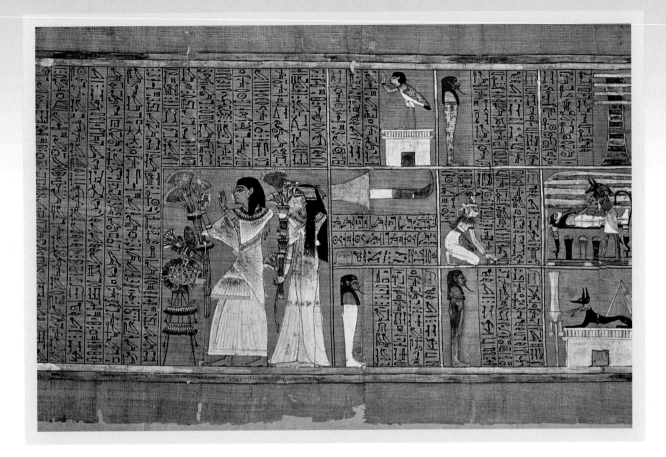

clothing, professions, and technologies of their times. Thanks to Egypt's dry climate, these bright, vividly colored pictures have survived the ravages of the centuries.

The records of the ancient Egyptians communicate their beliefs about family, work, life, and death—the same concerns that are important to us today. As the Egyptologist Geoffrey T. Martin wrote, "We should always remember that the ancient Egyptians were real human beings susceptible to all of the emotions, as we know from many written and pictorial sources, that are the common lot of mankind."

The Egyptians' written records have taught us a great deal about their beliefs and way of life.

CHAPTER ONE

THE RISE AND FALL OF THE ANCIENT EGYPTIANS

The development of ancient Egyptian civilization was greatly shaped by Egypt's two most important geographical features—the Nile River and the desert surrounding it. The Nile runs northward from deep in the African continent 4,130 miles (6,647 kilometers) to the Mediterranean Sea. It is the longest river in the world. In southern and central Egypt, it flows through a narrow valley in the highlands. This region is called Upper Egypt or the Nile valley. The low-lying area where the Nile empties into the Mediterranean is called Lower Egypt or the Nile delta.

Each year, the mighty Nile flooded when melting snows and heavy rainfall in the mountains of central Africa swelled the river. The river overflowed its banks, depositing layers of rich black soil and life-providing water to the dry desert sands at its sides. The Egyptians called their country Kemet, or the "black land," after the rich, dark mud and soil that was deposited in the valley and

delta areas. They called the barren, infertile land beyond the river Deshret, or the "red land."

The earliest Egyptians began settling in Upper and Lower Egypt by 4000 BCE. The inhabitants of these small villages and settlements often worked together to build reservoirs and irrigation systems to increase the amount of farmable land.

Irrigation canals allowed Egyptian farmers to raise crops farther from the banks of the Nile.

UNITING THE TWO LANDS

Over time, several settlements throughout both Upper and Lower Egypt developed into centers of power. These power centers traded with one another and fought for control of surrounding

Though Menes may not have been a real person, he is an important symbol of Egypt's unification.

nomes (NOHMZ) provinces, or districts, in ancient Egypt

vizier (vih-ZEER) an ancient Egyptian civil officer with important decision-making powers

lands. Today's scholars are unsure of the exact histories of these settlements, as many of their remains are still buried beneath thick layers of soil.

The ancient Egyptians have their own explanation of how these many independent civilizations united to become one. According to this interpretation of history, the settlements of Upper Egypt and Lower Egypt eventually organized into two separate kingdoms. These independent kingdoms were called the Two Lands. The kingdoms became bitter enemies, often raiding each other's territory. In about 3100 BCE, Upper Egypt conquered Lower Egypt. Menes, the ruler of Upper Egypt, united the Two Lands, merging them into a single, powerful state. To better govern the entire country, Menes moved his capital from the south to Memphis, where the two kingdoms met. He appointed government officials whose job it was to oversee the many provinces, or **nomes**, that had been established. He also selected a chief administrator, called a **vizier**, who was similar to a modern-day prime minister. The position of vizier remained essential throughout Egypt's history.

THE INFLUENCE OF THE PHARAOHS

Egyptian Revival is a style of architecture that uses themes and imagery borrowed from ancient Egypt. The style has flourished twice in modern times: from 1830 to 1850, following Napoleon Bonaparte's conquest of Egypt in 1798; and in the 1920s and 1930s, following the discovery of Tutankhamen's tomb in 1922. The style has mainly been used in public and educational buildings, churches, theaters, cemeteries, and memorials. Egyptian Revival flourished in the United States and Great Britain, and many of those buildings still stand today.

One of the newest and most spectacular examples of Egyptian Revival is the Supreme Constitutional Court of Egypt in Cairo. Another famous example is the Washington Monument, in Washington, D.C. Designed during the mid-1800s, it is shaped like an **obelisk** and was formerly decorated with Egyptian-influenced designs.

Modern scholars are unsure whether or not Menes was a real person. What we know of him comes from the written historical records of ancient Egypt. Many historians believe that the authors of these records created Menes in an attempt to simplify a long and complicated history. Real or mythical, Menes is considered the first pharaoh of Egypt, although Egyptians did not use that term until about 1,700 years later. His rule began the concept of dynasties, or royal families, in Egypt. To date, Egyptologists—the scholars, researchers, and archaeologists who study Egypt—have identified thirty dynasties.

Viziers and other officials served as important advisers to the pharaohs.

obelisks (OB-uh-lisks) tapering, four-sided shafts of stone, usually having a pointed top

mastabas (MAS-ta-bas) Egyptian tombs that are rectangular in shape with sloped sides and a flat roof

EARLY DYNASTIC PERIOD: A CIVILIZATION DEVELOPS

The Early Dynastic Period extended from about 3200 to 2700 BCE. Little is known about this period, but Egyptologists have determined that it was an important time of early Egyptian development. Much of what we do know about Early Dynastic leaders comes from their mud brick tombs at Abydos (in Upper Egypt) and the **mastabas** at Saqqara (a few miles from Memphis). Mastabas have flat tops and sloping sides and were built aboveground.

Menes and the pharaohs that followed him established their power mainly by asserting themselves as absolute rulers. They considered themselves divine beings, the physical forms of the gods the Egyptians worshipped.

Despite occasional rebellions against the kings, early Egyptian civilization flourished. Hieroglyphs developed. A paperlike substance called papyrus was invented. It was made from the flattened and dried papyrus plant, which grew in abundance in Lower Egypt. Egyptians looked to the skies and studied the movement of stars, eventually inventing the 12-month calendar similar to the one we use today.

Mastabas were an early stepping-stone toward the massive pyramids the Egyptians would later build.

The pharaohs oversaw huge public works projects, building a large system of canals and water basins to irrigate the fields along the Nile. This provided a plentiful food supply to feed the growing nation. Additionally, the efficient administration of Egypt's nomes and kingdoms by the early pharaohs created political stability.

THE OLD KINGDOM: THE AGE OF THE PYRAMIDS

The Third through Sixth Dynasties of Egypt comprise the Old Kingdom, which spanned from roughly 2770 to 2200 BCE. This era is often called the Age of the Pyramids because it was during this time that the Egyptians developed the pyramid, the world's most enduring monumental structure.

Pharaoh Djoser (reigned ca. 2691–2663 BCE), the first king of the Third Dynasty, turned to his vizier, Imhotep (ca. 2650–2600 BCE), to design his tomb at Saqqara. Imhotep devised an ingenious plan in which six stone mastabas were stacked on top of one another. Each mastaba was slightly smaller than the one below it, creating steps from the rising mastabas. The world's first pyramid-tomb came to be called the Step Pyramid.

Imhotep revolutionized building construction in the ancient world. The Step Pyramid was an innovative feat of engineering. Never before had stone been used in a structure of that size. Until that time, only mud brick was used as a material for a royal tomb. Imhotep's design paved the way for the construction of colossal tombs for Egypt's royalty.

It was not until the beginning of the Fourth Dynasty, however, that pyramid builders began filling in the steps of the pyramids to create a true, or smooth-sided, pyramid. Sneferu (reigned ca. 2613–2589 BCE), the first pharaoh of the Fourth Dynasty, is believed to have ordered the construction of the first true pyramid. However, he most likely claimed the pyramid at Meidum built by Huni, the last pharaoh of the Third Dynasty, and filled in the seven steps with limestone. Sneferu is also credited with building two pyramids in Dahshur, near present-day Cairo.

Sneferu was succeeded by his son, Khufu (reigned ca. 2589–2566 BCE), and grandson, Khafre (reigned ca. 2558–2532 BCE). They, too, ordered the construction of pyramids. Khufu's Great Pyramid is the largest of the three pyramids that stand at the Giza Plateau, northwest of Memphis. The massive structure originally towered 481 feet (147 meters) high and covered 13 acres (5 hectares) of land. Roughly 2.3 million blocks of limestone cut from nearby quarries were used in its construction. The Great Pyramid was the tallest man-made structure in the world for 3,800 years, until it was surpassed by the 525-foot (160 m) spire of Lincoln Cathedral in England. Khafre's pyramid at Giza was slightly smaller, measuring 471 feet (144 m) tall. The pyramid-tombs of father and

This ivory statue of Khufu was found at the tombs of Abydos.

son were part of a larger complex that included smaller pyramids, temples, and causeways leading to other structures.

The enormity of the pyramids was meant to indicate the importance of the pharaohs who were buried within them. Egyptians of the Fourth Dynasty viewed their rulers as divine beings worthy of massive tombs. Despite their seemingly impenetrable construction, however, most of the pyramid-tombs were eventually broken into and robbed of their treasures.

The Great Pyramid is one of the most recognizable landmarks in the world.

For centuries, many people believed that the pyramids were built by slaves. In recent years, Egyptologists have discovered this belief to be false. Since 1988, archaeologist Mark Lehner has directed the Giza Plateau Mapping Project near the Giza pyramids. The project has unearthed what seems to have been a town for workers who helped build the pyramids. Experts now believe that the pyramid workforce was a combination of experienced stonecutters and other skilled laborers working with local farmers and villagers. The laborers willingly came to Giza to work for their kings and build their tombs. The discoveries shed light on the lifestyle of the pyramid builders and helped to disprove the myth that workers were poorly treated slaves forced to work against their will.

The era of massive pyramid building came to an end with the passing of the Fourth Dynasty. Pharaohs of the Fifth and Sixth Dynasties continued to build pyramids, but those pyramids were smaller and poorly constructed.

Archaeological digs at Giza have helped us learn about how the pyramids were constructed.

As the central government saw its authority slip away, the Old Kingdom government grew weaker. A series of devastating droughts, in which the Nile flooded less than usual, destroyed crop production. The final years of the Sixth Dynasty were marked by civil unrest, famine, and economic chaos. One of the last pharaohs of the Old Kingdom was Pepi II (reigned ca. 2246–2152 BCE), who ruled for more than ninety years. The Old Kingdom collapsed shortly after his death.

First Intermediate Period: A Nation Divided

The First Intermediate Period, spanning from 2200 to 2050 BCE, followed the decline of the Old Kingdom. It included the Seventh to mid-Eleventh Dynasties. By the Seventh and Eighth Dynasties, Egypt had broken into numerous small warring states. The authority of the pharaohs was limited to Memphis and nearby regions.

During the Ninth and Tenth Dynasties, the pharaohs of Memphis began to reassert their influence, taking control of much of Lower Egypt and the northern portion of Upper Egypt by roughly 2160 BCE. In the south, a group of competing pharaohs arose at Thebes during the Eleventh Dynasty.

The pharaohs in Memphis and Thebes were rival rulers, controlling their own territories at the same time. In about 2060 BCE, the Theban prince Mentuhotep II conquered his northern rivals and reunited the nation. He crushed rebellions, reestablished political stability, and rebuilt the economy. His efforts set the stage for Egypt's second era of prosperity and accomplishment—the Middle Kingdom.

THE MIDDLE KINGDOM: A REBIRTH OF PAST GLORIES

Spanning roughly four hundred years from 2050 to 1650 BCE, the Middle Kingdom includes the second half of the Eleventh Dynasty, the Twelfth Dynasty, and the beginning of the Thirteenth Dynasty. Choosing the name "He who unites the Two Lands," Mentuhotep II led a rebirth of Egypt's past glory. Seeking to extend Egypt's borders, he took control of northern Nubia, not far from Aswan, in present-day Sudan. There, he gained control over important trade routes, increasing foreign trade and gaining access to raw materials.

Amenemhat, the first pharaoh of the Twelfth Dynasty, moved the capital from Memphis to nearby Itjtawy, a spot more centrally located in the country. Succeeding pharaohs reorganized local governments, making sure to limit their powers and thus strengthening the central government.

The rulers of the Twelfth Dynasty were often bold visionaries who undertook major building projects, including the earliest portions of the largest temple complex ever built—the Temple at Karnak, dedicated to the god Amun. Senusret II (reigned ca. 1880–1874 BCE) instituted a huge expansion of farmlands. The pharaohs of the Middle Kingdom also encouraged education for the upper class and adopted progressive legal concepts such as forgiveness and justice.

Mentuhotep II led ancient Egypt from the First Intermediate Period into the Middle Kingdom.

SECOND INTERMEDIATE PERIOD: INTERNAL UNREST

As Egypt appeared to be on the threshold of its greatest achievements, the nation fell into yet another period of chaos, known as the Second Intermediate Period. This era of foreign invasion and internal division spanned one hundred years, from 1650 to 1550 BCE, and included the Thirteenth to Seventeenth Dynasties.

Decades prior to the collapse of the Middle Kingdom, people from Palestine and Syria to the east had begun settling in the Nile delta. The Egyptians called these peoples Hyksos, or "rulers of foreign lands." As weak pharaohs once again allowed the central

Many statues and structures still stand at the ruins of the Temple of Amun at Karnak.

government to lose power to local nobles, the Hyksos took control of the Nile delta and much of Lower Egypt. In the south, Egyptian pharaohs held on to power in Thebes, and the Hyksos did not interfere with them. The Hyksos collected **tribute**, or payments, from their subjects, but otherwise left the Egyptians to tend to their own affairs.

The Hyksos blended into Egyptian culture, adopting the traditional clothes and customs of their conquered subjects. They built a new capital in the eastern Nile delta and established the Fifteenth and Sixteenth Dynasties.

After what they saw as a century of foreign occupation, Egyptian leaders in Thebes rose up against the Hyksos and began driving them out of the country back into Syria and Palestine. Led by Ahmose, the founder of the Eighteenth Dynasty, the Egyptians achieved victory with the aid of a new military innovation—the **chariot**, which had been introduced by the Hyksos.

The one hundred years of Hyksos domination taught the Egyptians that they were not safe from foreign influence. To protect themselves, they had to take the upper hand against neighboring civilizations. Egypt's age of empire expansion was ready to begin.

The Hyksos were finally driven from Egypt at the beginning of the Eighteenth Dynasty.

tribute (TRIB-yoot) payment given as a sign of respect

chariot (CHAR-ee-uht) a small vehicle pulled by a horse, used in ancient times in battles or for racing

The New Kingdom: The Age of the Empire

Ahmose reunified the Two Lands, beginning the period known as the New Kingdom (1550–1070 BCE). The New Kingdom incorporated the Eighteenth to Twentieth Dynasties, marking Egypt's greatest period of domestic stability and prosperity. Egypt embarked on a campaign of empire building, expanding into territories on the might of their well-trained army and rapidly developing navy. Within one hundred years of Ahmose's death, the Egyptian Empire stretched from the southern Nile all the way to the Euphrates River in the east.

Chariots quickly became one of the Egyptian military's most important tools.

Egyptian expansion created enormous wealth in the nation. Defeated states paid tributes to their Egyptian conquerors. By taking control of new trade routes in distant lands, the Egyptians grew their commercial interests. They also gained access to valuable natural resources such as much-needed timber and gold. With this newfound wealth, Egypt turned once again to building mammoth statues, monuments, and temples. Art and architecture flourished there as never before.

Hatshepsut (reigned ca. 1473-1458 BCE) was one of Egypt's few female rulers. She made a lasting impact on the development of trade and industry in her country. Hatshepsut sponsored an important trade expedition to the land of Punt, in present-day Somalia, and her representatives brought back large quantities of foreign goods, most importantly incense. Incense was used in large quantities during ceremonies for the gods, but was impossible to grow in Egypt because of the climate. Hatshepsut's temple in Deir el-Bahari near Thebes features carvings of scenes from the expedition. Hatshepsut also oversaw many building projects, including the rebuilding of temples that had been destroyed by the Hyksos.

Thutmose III (reigned 1479–1426 BCE) succeeded Hatshepsut on the throne. He immediately organized military campaigns that expanded Egypt's borders. His victory over the Mitannians at Megiddo in southern Syria earned him comparisons to Alexander the Great in later centuries.

Another noteworthy New Kingdom pharaoh was Akhenaten (reigned ca. 1353–1336 BCE), whose views on religion almost destroyed the Eighteenth Dynasty. Akhenaten tried to replace the Egyptians' worship of many gods with one supreme deity—Aten, the supreme force of light. When he closed down temples dedicated

Thanks to his incredible tomb and famous burial mask, Tutankhamen is one of the most recognizable pharaohs among people today.

to Amun, the primary Egyptian god, he angered the priesthood, causing a rift in Egyptian society. Akhenaten relocated the capital of Egypt from Memphis to Akhetaten, where he could practice his religious beliefs. But he failed to protect Egypt's borders, and foreign forces gained control of Egypt's territories in Syria. Akhenaten was succeeded by the most famous of all Egyptian pharaohs, King Tutankhamen (ca. 1341–1323 BCE). Only eight years old when he took the throne, Tutankhamen moved the capital city back to Memphis. However, his fame does not come from his achievements but rather from the discovery of his magnificent tomb in 1922 by English archaeologist Howard Carter. Tutankhamen's major contribution to Egyptian culture was reestablishing the worship of many gods, which his father, King Akhenaten, had rejected years earlier.

Seti I, the second king of the Nineteenth Dynasty (reigned ca. 1290–1279 BCE), attempted to reestablish Egypt as the world's most feared empire. He invaded territories in the eastern Mediterranean region, capturing important port cities. Seti also battled a people called the Hittites in southern Syria. His failure to remove the Hittites from Syria soon became a problem for his son, Ramses II (ca. 1303–1213 BCE), who succeeded him.

Ramses II, also known as Ramses the Great, is considered one of ancient Egypt's most powerful monarchs. Reigning from 1279 to 1213 BCE, he was one of the empire's most prolific builders, erecting numerous temples, palaces, and monuments throughout the nation. He also built a new capital city at Pi-Ramesses, southeast of the Nile delta. The capital was home to the king's palace, temples, gardens, and even a zoo.

He had one of the largest families in royal history, with many wives and as many as fifty sons and daughters. The powerful pharaoh urged his people to honor him as a god by placing countless statues of himself in temples throughout the nation.

The reign of Ramses II was the second longest in Egyptian history.

In 1275 BCE, Ramses II attempted to do what his father could not: rid Egypt of the Hittite threat. An army of eighteen thousand infantrymen and two thousand chariots marched to Kadesh in southern Syria. The foes fought for hours in the largest chariot battle ever waged. Each side claimed victory, but there was no clear winner. In about 1259 BCE, the two nations signed a peace treaty,

Ramses the Great led the Egyptian forces against the Hittites at the Battle of Kadesh.

ending the hostilities. The Hittite civilization soon fell into decline, rapidly losing its status as an important regional power.

During the late Nineteenth and Twentieth Dynasties, threats from foreign invaders, climate change, and population movements began to undermine Egypt's stability. The Sea Peoples, groups of displaced peoples from the Balkans, Black Sea, and Mediterranean regions of Europe, periodically launched attacks on Egypt. Although the Egyptians, led by Ramses III (reigned ca. 1187–1156 BCE), successfully fought off the invaders, the attacks left the nation in a weakened state. From the south, Nubians pushed toward the Nile delta, reclaiming lands that Egypt had seized from them. In Syria, the Assyrians conquered the Hittites and replaced them as the dominant power in the region. Armed with iron weapons, stronger than the Egyptian's bronze weapons, the Assyrians also invaded Egypt.

Periods of drought led to crop failures, which in turn forced people living in Libya, west of Egypt, to migrate into the Nile valley. The Egyptians found themselves surrounded by foreigners and foes, and they lost control of their eastern Mediterranean lands and the valuable natural resources they provided. Coupled with a series of weak Twentieth Dynasty pharaohs, the New Kingdom collapsed. By 1070 BCE, Egypt's government was in chaos and the empire had been lost.

The Assyrians used advanced weapons when they invaded Egypt.

The Libyan pharaoh Sheshonk was the first ruler of the Twenty-Second Dynasty.

THIRD INTERMEDIATE PERIOD AND LATE PERIOD: THE TARGET OF FOREIGN INVADERS

Torn apart by civil unrest, Egypt slumped into the final centuries of dynastic rulership, known as the Third Intermediate (1070–663 BCE) and Late Periods (663–332 BCE). During the Twenty-First Dynasty, two new groups rose to power. Priests ruled Upper Egypt from Thebes, while a wealthy family ruled from Tanis, a city in Lower Egypt. Each group claimed to have the rightful pharaoh to the throne. The weakened nation was now even more vulnerable to foreign attacks.

In about 950 BCE, Libyans took control of the Nile delta. A Libyan ruler declared himself pharaoh and reunited Upper and Lower Egypt for a brief period. But civil unrest once again tore the nation apart as rival leaders fought for power during the Twenty-Third and Twenty-Fourth Dynasties.

A line of competent Nubian rulers gained control in the Twenty-Fifth Dynasty, the start of the Late Period. However, they were unable to reunite the nation or defend its borders against foreign attack. In about 670 BCE, King Esarhaddon of Assyria launched an attack on northern Egypt. The powerful armies of the Assyrian Empire quickly subdued the lands around Memphis.

Esarhaddon drove out the Nubians but was unable to overcome the fierce resistance put up by Egyptian forces.

Esarhaddon appointed Egyptian governors to oversee his affairs in the conquered land. When Esarhaddon's successor, Assurbanipal, withdrew Assyrian troops from Egypt in 670 BCE, the governors assumed leadership of the country. One of the governors, Psammetichus, was based in Sais in the western Nile delta. Facing

King Esarhaddon of Assyria conquered Egypt in 670 BCE.

little resistance, he was able to take control of the entire nation, reuniting it once again. Psammetichus I was the first of the Saite rulers. His leadership marks the beginning of the Twenty-Sixth Dynasty, a period of about one hundred years of relative peace, prosperity, and unity.

Saite armies, however, were no match for the next onslaught of foreign invaders—the powerful Persian Empire. In 525 BCE, the Persians swept into Egypt, easily crushing the Egyptian resistance. This began the Twenty-Seventh Dynasty, also known as the Persian Period.

Despite several rebellions against the Persians, the Egyptians were unable to rid their country of the invaders. When Macedonian-Greek commander Alexander III (356–323 BCE) marched his forces into the Nile valley in 332 BCE, the Egyptians actually welcomed him as a liberator from the Persians. They soon learned, however, that Alexander had no plans of freeing them.

Alexander III is regarded as one of history's greatest military leaders.

PTOLEMAIC PERIOD: THE FINAL CHAPTER

Alexander built a magnificent seaport city, Alexandria, on the shores of the Mediterranean Sea. It eventually became one of the world's leading cultural and commercial centers. After the city was built, Alexander left Egypt to conquer the rest of the Persian Empire. He left troops behind to control Egypt.

When Alexander died in 323 BCE, Ptolemy, one of his leading generals, seized control of Egypt. Ptolemy founded a new dynasty, ushering in the

Ptolemaic Period. For the next three hundred years, the Ptolemies ruled Egypt, spreading Greek influences and customs throughout the country. During this time, the Roman Empire was expanding its sphere of influence, conquering numerous Greek territories and lands in the Mediterranean.

Cleopatra VII (69–30 BCE) was the last independent Ptolemaic ruler. Intelligent and ambitious—and hoping to restore the glory of Egypt—she developed relationships with two of Rome's leading figures, Julius Caesar and Mark Antony. In 31 BCE, however, Cleopatra and Mark Antony were defeated by Roman forces in a naval battle at Actium in western Greece. The next year, Cleopatra committed suicide, allegedly by the bite of a poisonous snake. Her death ended the 3,200-year reign of the Egyptian pharaohs. Egypt became a province of Rome and remained under Roman control until the fourth century CE.

Cleopatra played a major role in the history of both Egypt and Rome.

CHAPTER TWO

GOVERNING THE KINGDOM

T he structure and functions of government in ancient Egypt were greatly influenced by religion. In fact, government and religion were nearly inseparable.

A pharaoh kneels before the god Amun-Ra.

The pharaohs' power was based on the Egyptians' belief that their ruler spoke with the blessings of the gods. The pharaoh was viewed as protector and guardian of the country. Egypt could prosper only if the people obeyed him. The pharaoh's responsibility to his subjects was to make certain that he maintained proper order and stability, or **ma'at**, throughout the land.

Viewed as sons of the sun god Ra, pharaohs were perhaps the most powerful rulers in world history. Egyptians feared each pharaoh and the control he held over them. People bowed before him, and few were even allowed to look at him directly unless he granted them permission.

The pharaoh's authority was limitless. Egyptians believed that he owned everything—the land and all that lived on it, including the people. During much of Egypt's history, no one owned private property. The pharaoh sometimes gave someone permission to run a farm or village, but everything produced by that person's labor belonged to the pharaoh. Little by little, though, the pharaohs gave up control of their land. If a family had managed a farm for a long time, for example, the land was sometimes given to them. The pharaoh, however, still had the power to tax the farm's production. Pharaohs also donated a great deal of land to temples in order to gain the support of Theban priests. After centuries of these practices, temples and small farmers collectively held more land than the pharaoh did.

Priests were very influential in ancient Egyptian society.

ma'at (MAY-eht) the ancient Egyptian concept of justice, order, and goodness; Ma'at was the goddess who embodied those virtues

GOVERNING A NATION

The pharaoh was an essential part of the Egyptian government, but he could not oversee its operation without considerable help from many other officials. During the early dynasties, pharaohs' sons were often appointed to important government positions. It was common for a prince to be named engineer of his father's pyramid and temple, or supervisor of public works projects such as irrigation systems, reservoirs, or roadways. As Egypt prospered and its population grew, however, pharaohs began hiring people outside of the royal family as government officials. By the end of the great pyramid-building years of the Old Kingdom, a pharaoh's children often became priests or priestesses instead of serving in the government.

NATIVE TONGUES

Even though Egyptologists could not read the written language of the ancient Egyptians until relatively recently, traces of the ancient spoken language have long been a part of the Arabic spoken by modern Egyptians. After Egypt was conquered by the Arabs in the 600s, Egyptians slowly began adopting the Arabic language. However, many of their traditional words and phrases survived the transition. Egyptians simply kept using them because those words and phrases

were able to express certain ideas better than the Arabic language could. Egyptians also adapted certain Arabic words and phrases to fit in with concepts. For example, Egyptians are the only Arabic-speaking people to use the Arabic word for "life" to mean "bread." This practice is rooted in the ancient Egyptian language, where one word was used for both life and bread.

At the height of the Egyptian Empire, the government consisted of three branches. One oversaw civil affairs. Another supervised the temples and clergy. The third managed the pharaoh's landholdings and royal court.

THE FUNCTION OF CIVIL GOVERNMENT

Each branch of the government established a rigid chain of command in which the pharaoh's wishes could be communicated to ordinary citizens through local leaders. The highest position in civil government was the vizier. It is believed that one vizier was appointed in the north and one in the south. The vizier's main duty was to carry out the wishes of the pharaoh, whether it was to ensure the ma'at of the judicial system or to organize the construction of buildings. Beneath the vizier were ministers, who were responsible for maintaining the nation's treasury, collecting taxes, and supervising the courts.

Egypt was divided into forty-two nomes. Each nome was supervised by a nomarch, who sometimes wielded the power of a local king. Each nomarch was assisted by town mayors, law enforcement officials, and local councils called *kenbets*. The nomarch appointed the members of each kenbet. The kenbets served as Egypt's court system, deciding on most issues of law, including property disputes and criminal cases. Kenbets were given broad powers to carry out their decisions. They could seize property and give it to the winner of a judgment, or order physical punishment. There were no prisons in Egypt, so serious offenders were often sentenced to hard labor or exiled to outlying territories.

A treasury official oversaw the collection of taxes, which were usually paid in the form of grain, leather, meat, minerals, or textiles. Every citizen in the nation had to pay taxes. The tax rate on farmers

was generally set at 10 percent of what they should have produced, based on the height of that year's flooding of the Nile. People who refused to pay their taxes were often beaten or jailed. To maximize the amount of taxes it could collect, the government kept the irrigation systems and reservoirs in good condition. This responsibility was given to the supervisors of the nomes.

Beneath the treasury official were overseers of grain production and cattle. Their job was to supply the military and feed the many workers building Egypt's pyramids, monuments, and public works projects.

GOVERNING THE RELIGIOUS ESTABLISHMENT

One of the pharaoh's primary roles in Egyptian society was to serve as the nation's high priest. To perform this duty in a land as vast as Egypt, he appointed a priest to act as his representative in each temple. As Egypt flourished, thousands of temples sprang up throughout the country. Each god had one main temple dedicated to him or her. The more important gods also had several smaller temples. Pharaohs built temples to preserve their own memories, and wealthy families constructed statues at temples to preserve the memory of their departed relatives. In time, tens of thousands of people worked in Egypt's religious establishment.

To manage this vast priestly network, the pharaoh appointed an overseer to supervise the temples and priests. Often, a vizier acted as the overseer of the temples, in addition to his other civic duties. Below the overseer were high priests, each one representing a god of Egypt.

Each individual temple employed a chief priest, and larger temples often had several priests who served under him. Lower

Livestock were a valuable resource in ancient Egypt.

clergymen were divided into two job functions. Scroll carriers cared for and read the holy writings of the temple. Wab priests cared for the temple's sacred objects, such as idols. Scroll carriers and wab priests were male, but women could serve as priestesses, singing or dancing for a god. Each temple employed workers who made clothing for the priests and cooked for the temple staff. Priests were usually paid with crops grown on temple-owned lands.

Temples were an essential part of Egypt's economy. The wealthiest and most powerful temples were located in the capital cities of Thebes and Memphis. Temples received a steady stream of income from three primary sources: gifts from the pharaoh, income from the temples' considerable land and livestock holdings, and donations by individuals. Temple records at the time of Ramses III (reigned ca. 1187–1156 BCE) indicate that temples owned about one-third of all the farmable land in Egypt.

OVERSEEING THE ROYAL COURT

The pharaoh employed thousands of workers to manage his estates and work on his land. A governor of the palace and officials beneath him supervised the activities at the king's multiple palaces. Guards, cooks and servants, gardeners, entertainers, and craftsmen staffed each palace complex. Dozens of statesmen and **scribes** oversaw matters of foreign affairs from offices near the royal complex.

A large staff of attendants cared for the pharaoh's personal needs. The overseer of royal clothing supervised a group that included a washer, a rober, and a fabric bleacher. The staff also included wig makers, barbers, bathers, and sandal bearers. A team of doctors and magicians specializing in different illnesses cared for the pharaoh's health.

The pharaoh's children lived in a separate part of the palace, away from the adults. They were raised by royal nurses, who tutored them and tended to their daily needs. Many royal nurses were female relatives of trusted government officials.

scribes (SKRIBZ) people who copy books, letters, contracts, and other documents by hand

CHAPTER THREE

A LAND OF PLENTY

About twelve thousand years ago, grasslands covered most of North Africa. Many animal species grazed on the lands. As the region's climate became drier, these grasslands turned to sandy deserts. Through this desert, the Nile River flowed

The Egyptians grazed cattle and other animals in the fertile area along the banks of the Nile.

northward along its long, narrow valley, making its way to the Mediterranean Sea. Without the Nile, Egypt could not exist.

The ancient Egyptians praised and worshipped the Nile, believing that their existence depended on it. In the hymn "The Adoration of the Nile," Egyptians sang, "Praise to thee, O Nile, that issue from the earth, and come to nourish Egypt!" They glorified Hapi, the god of the Nile's flooding, as "the bringer of food, rich in provisions, creator of all good."

THE RIVER NILE

The Nile is formed by two branches: the Blue Nile, which flows west from Ethiopia; and the White Nile, which flows north from Lake Victoria. The White Nile and Blue Nile meet at present-day

Regular flooding brought important nutrients from the Nile to the surrounding soil.

The Nile stretches for hundreds of miles.

Khartoum in Sudan. In six places along the river, rocks and small boulders fill the riverbed. These spots are called **cataracts**, where rapid currents of water rush around the rocks, making it impossible for ships to pass.

The Nile region is composed of two main parts, the valley and the delta, which correspond to the ancient division of the country into Upper and Lower Egypt. The Nile valley is a long canyon that runs for about 650 miles (1,046 km). Most of the Nile flows through flat plains known as the floodplain. The floodplain occupies about 4,250 square miles (11,000 sq km) and ranges in width from roughly 1 mile (1.6 km) to 11 miles (17.7 km).

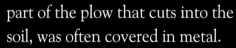

The Past Is Present
DIG THIS!

Evidence suggests that the Egyptians were among the first civilizations to use plows, in roughly 4000 BCE. Early plows were lightweight and made of wood. They were often modified hand tools used by a single person, and could not dig very deep into the ground. Teams of people pulled larger plows. In about 2000 BCE, Egyptians began using oxen to pull the plows. The earliest plow designs connected to the cattle's horns, but this interfered with the animals' breathing. Improved versions used a system of leather straps, which were more effective. The share, the part of the plow that cuts into the soil, was often covered in metal.

Today, the concept of plowing in general is integral to modern farming everywhere. Though basic plows similar to those used by the Egyptians are still used in some parts of the world, most farmers use modern versions that are pulled by tractors and can plow many rows at once.

The floodplain is Egypt's most fertile farmland. Every year, rains and snowmelt high in the Ethiopian mountains caused the Nile to swell, flooding the plains from June to October. During this time, ancient Egyptian farmers anxiously waited for the floodwaters to recede. When they did, the water left behind thousands of square miles of rich soil from the Nile's riverbed. The flooding of the Nile, called the inundation, assured the Egyptians they would have enough to eat in the coming year.

The strength of the inundation, however, was not the same every year. A "low" Nile flooded only part of the plains, and not enough crops could be grown to feed the people. During years of a low Nile, water shortages often resulted in outbreaks of disease and civil unrest. A "high" Nile threatened villages and towns with devastating floods. Fearing this, many ancient Egyptian settlements were built as far from the riverbanks as possible.

As it continues its journey northward, the Nile splits near Cairo into two branches that flow into the Mediterranean. The mud and **silt** deposited between the branches forms a massive triangle of fertile soil, creating the Nile delta. Roughly 100 miles long (161 km), the delta covers 8,500 square miles (22,000 km), spanning about 150 miles (241 km) across at its widest point on the coast. The soil of the delta was among the most fertile in ancient Egypt.

THE DESERT SANDS

The Nile divides northern Africa's vast Sahara Desert into Egypt's Western and Eastern Deserts. These were the arid territories the ancient Egyptians called Deshret, or the "red land." The sprawling Western Desert covers about two-thirds of present-day Egypt. It is believed that the earliest Egyptian civilization began in the

silt (SILT) fine particles of soil carried by flowing water that settle to the bottom of a river or lake

southwestern region of the Western Desert. As the region became drier, the cattle herders left the area and migrated toward the Nile valley. There, the seeds of Egyptian society and religion took root. The mountainous Eastern Desert is also known as the Arabian Desert. Nestling against the shores of the Red Sea, it was a rich source of minerals in ancient times.

Valley dwellers believed the deserts were dangerous places. However, they were not entirely deadly. Throughout the Western Desert were **oases**, small areas with water and plants. Dry river-beds called **wadis** ran through the Eastern Desert, making them ideal trade routes across the desert to the Red Sea. After a heavy downpour, the wadis filled with rain, which provided traders, travelers, and their pack animals a source of water.

Wadis provided convenient travel routes through harsh desert areas.

oases (oh-AY-sees) places in a desert where there is water aboveground and plants can grow

wadis (WAH-deez) dry valleys in a desert region

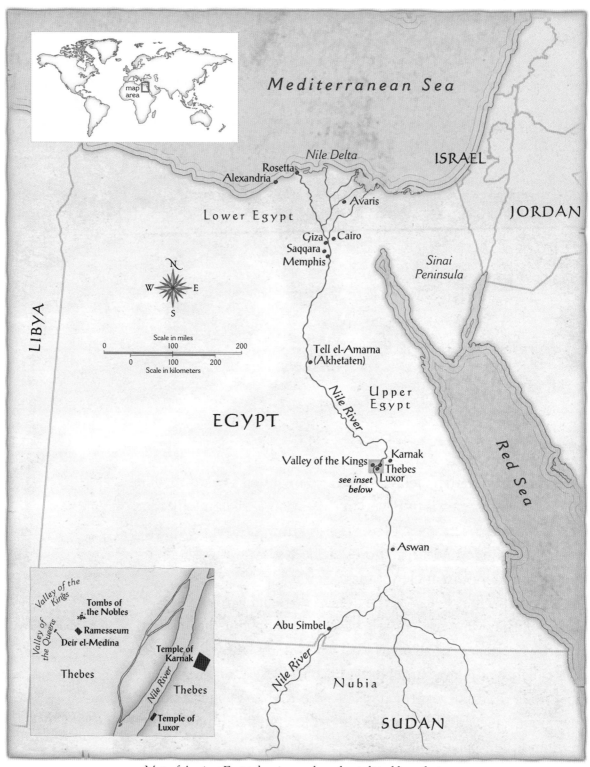

Map of Ancient Egypt showing modern-day political boundaries

CLIMATE

Egypt receives very little rain. Rainfall in most of the country
is about 3 inches (7.6 centimeters) per year, although the delta
region may receive as much as 8 inches (20.3 cm) annually.
Winter lasts from November to April, and summer from May to
October. Average winter temperatures in the deserts can be as
low as 32 degrees Fahrenheit (0 degrees Celsius) at night and as
high as 65°F (18°C) during the day. In the summer, average desert
temperatures vary greatly, ranging from 45°F (7°C) at night to
104°F (40°C) during the day. Along the coast in the delta, daytime
temperatures range between an average minimum of 57°F (14°C)
in winter and an average maximum of 86°F (30°C) in summer.

*Just as they are today,
summers in ancient
Egypt were often
extremely hot.*

With so little rain, ancient Egyptian farmers had to use the waters of the inundation with great care. They invented a system of basins and canals to store the water, and then released it into their fields when it was needed.

THE FRUITS OF THE NILE

Farmers harvested their crops from February to mid-June, when the Nile had receded and was at its lowest. They grew a wide variety of plants, including wheat and barley, from which bread and cakes were made. Barley was also used to make a nutritious beer, usually sweetened with honey or dates. The Egyptian diet, mainly grain based, was supplemented by protein-containing foods such as beans and lentils. Vegetables such as lettuce, cucumbers, leeks, and onions were also eaten. Many types of herbs were cultivated for medicinal uses.

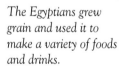

The Egyptians grew grain and used it to make a variety of foods and drinks.

Fruits grown in orchards included melons, dates, figs, and grapes, which were used to produce wine. Vineyard laborers picked grapes by hand and trampled them in large vats. The resulting juice was left in jugs for many weeks, allowing the sugar to ferment, or turn into alcohol.

Farmers also raised animals, mostly cattle, which grazed on the plentiful grasses in the delta. Because beef was not a major food source for the Egyptians, cattle were used for their milk and to plow the fields. People raised goats and pigs for meat. Poultry such as geese and ducks were raised for meat and eggs. Sheep provided a source of wool to make clothing and blankets. They were also a source of meat.

Papyrus helped change the way people kept records and passed messages to each other.

The Nile itself was a rich source of food, providing fish such as catfish and tilapia, which lived near the banks of the river among water reeds. Nile perch were caught in the irrigation ditches that led from the river to the crop fields.

The Nile also provided ancient Egyptians with valuable non-food resources. The flax plant was used to make rope and linen fabrics. The papyrus that grew in the marshes and swamps of the delta was used to make paperlike sheets. To make a sheet, papyrus stalks were sliced into thin, moist strips. A layer of horizontal strips was then placed on top of a layer of vertical strips. While still moist, the two layers were beaten together into a single sheet. The sheet was then dried and polished with a stone or round hard

The ancient Egyptians created mud bricks for use in their construction projects.

wood. Papyrus was also used to make rope, sandals, mats, mattresses, and boats. Mud from the Nile was used to make pottery and bricks.

FROM WITHIN THE EARTH

Ancient Egypt's large deposits of stone, metal, and minerals were widely mined. Most of these resources were found in the Eastern Desert and, in particular, along the shores of the Red Sea.

The desert hills on the edges of the Nile were a rich source of limestone, granite, and sandstone. These materials were used to build pyramids, temples, and monuments.

The Egyptians mined gold and copper from the earliest years of the Predynastic Period. The military usually supervised mining operations. Often, foreign workers made up the labor force.

Gold was mined primarily in the Eastern Desert between Thebes and Aswan, and in the Nubian Desert in southern Egypt. It was considered to be a divine substance. The flesh of the gods was believed to be made of gold, as evidenced by the use of gold in the death masks of the pharaohs. Covering the face of a dead pharaoh with a gold mask was an indication of the Egyptians' belief that their kings became gods after death. Gold was also used to adorn buildings, showing the structures' link to the worship of the Egyptian sun god, Ra. The tips of pyramids and obelisks were often covered with gold.

Copper, also mined in the Eastern Desert and Nubia, was used for small tools such as fishhooks and needles, decorative articles such as beads and rings, and cutting implements such as daggers and harpoons.

Semiprecious stones, such as amethyst, garnet, and feldspar, were mined in Upper Egypt. These stones were used to make a variety of beads, ornaments, and necklaces. Natron, an important mineral used to **mummify** dead bodies, was taken from Wadi el-Natrun south of Thebes.

Mining expeditions could number from a few hundred workers to more than ten thousand. Laborers of all types—craftsmen, stonecutters, miners, and unskilled workers—trekked into the arid desert regions in well-organized teams. They were supplied with food, water, and donkeys. The leader of the expedition carried a papyrus copy of the king's order that approved the mission. The commander often had the document inscribed on a rock wall near the mine. Archaeologists have found numerous work orders in mines describing where the work was done, how much stone or mineral was quarried, and how many men did the work.

mummify (MUH-mih-fye) to dry and preserve the body of a dead person or animal

CHAPTER FOUR

THE PULSE OF DAILY LIFE

M any historians and Egyptologists once believed that the ancient Egyptians were a grim and joyless people. These scholars viewed the rigid form of government and the frozen figures on ancient monuments as evidence that Egypt was a gloomy and formal civilization. A careful study of the evidence, however, suggests the opposite: the Egyptians were tolerant, easygoing, and filled with a joy for living. Isolated geographically from the outside world, Egypt developed with only limited contact with its neighbors. Lacking much outside influence, they created their own lifestyle. This isolation gave ancient Egypt its unique

The Egyptians' statues helped give them a reputation as an overly serious people.

character: self-reliant, optimistic, confident, and calm.

    The ancient Egyptians, like people today, worked hard, enjoyed family life, and found time to play games and sports. As Egyptologist Pierre Montet claims, "For the ordinary Egyptian, the good moments of life outnumbered the bad."

Wrestling was one of the many sports enjoyed by ancient Egyptians.

The Past Is Present

A SWEET SCIENCE

The Egyptians are believed to be the first people to domesticate, or raise, bees for honey and wax. A series of Old Kingdom temple carvings shows villagers removing a honeycomb from a beehive, pouring the honey into a storage vessel, and then putting the honey into pots with handles. Early man-made Egyptian hives were often made from bundles of reeds covered with mud. By the New Kingdom, hives consisted of cylinder-shaped vessels kept on their sides. The beekeeper smoked out the bees from the hive with burning candles, while an assistant

removed the combs. The emptied honeycombs were then crushed and boiled to make beeswax. The wax was used as a sealant in boatbuilding and for lining the insides of jars; in medicines; and in making paint.

Beeswax and honey remain important goods today. The wax can be found in everything from lip balm to protective outdoor clothing, and beekeepers around the world produce hundreds of millions of pounds of honey each year.

HOUSING

The size and layout of the typical ancient Egyptian house varied according to its owners' social status. Because most people were lower-class farmers and laborers, all they could afford were the simplest homes. Homes uncovered by archaeologists in the Amarna workmen's village in central Egypt usually consisted of three rooms. One room was used for doing work, another for socializing and sleeping, and the third for preparing food. People often kept smaller animals in their living quarters, overcrowding the already cramped conditions of the home. Larger animals lived on rooftops or outdoors.

The middle class was largely comprised of government officials, scribes, and army officers. Their higher incomes afforded them better living quarters. The finest homes were owned by Egypt's small upper

An Egyptian family's animals often lived on the flat rooftop of their home.

Wealthy Egyptians owned much more elaborate homes than commoners did.

class, which included nobles, royalty, and a few high priests. Most homes were made of mud brick. They were usually painted white on the inside and decorated with bright colors, pictures, and patterns on the outside.

Wealthy people sometimes constructed larger mansions and country estates. Estates in Amarna featured a large home and surrounding land enclosed within a mud brick or stone wall. The large homes had living rooms, reception halls, and bedrooms. Kitchens, stables, and servants housing were located in separate buildings from the main house.

Only the wealthy had bathrooms, but they were primitive at best. In a separate room attached to the bedroom, the user would squat over a pottery container filled with sand. Servants emptied the container after it was used. Without bathroom facilities, less wealthy Egyptians simply went to a private area in the house, relieved themselves into a pot, and dumped its contents outside.

The poorest living conditions were found in the most rural parts of the country on the outskirts of farmers' fields. There, homes were often made from branches and thick reeds. Many homes contained only one room, in which families and their animals lived together.

FAMILY LIFE

Marriage was the central feature of Egyptian family life. A couple married simply by agreeing to a contract that was negotiated between the man and the woman, or their families. The contract called for both sides to exchange gifts of equal value to establish the union of the couple. It also established what property belonged to each party and what property would be inherited by whom in case of death.

Although uncommon, divorce did occur. The marriage was dissolved by the man and woman by simply living apart. The original marriage contract outlined what would occur in the event of divorce. If a husband asked for the divorce, he returned the gifts he was given by the bride. If the wife requested the divorce, she would return half of her gifts to her husband. In either case, the husband was required to financially support his wife until she remarried.

Marriage contracts also included information about divorce procedures for the ancient Egyptians.

Regardless of social or economic status, children were important to the ancient Egyptians. Within Egypt's royalty, power passed from parent to child. In middle- and working-class families, sons were taught their fathers' trades, usually before the age of ten. Couples who could not have their own children often adopted a male orphan or servant. Sons had the responsibility of caring for their elderly parents and making funeral arrangements upon their death. Young girls helped their mothers around the house by cleaning, cooking, and making clothes.

WOMEN IN SOCIETY

Women were often responsible for grinding corn into flour.

Egyptian women enjoyed a high degree of personal and economic freedom for their era. Several women served as pharaohs, and female relatives of kings occasionally influenced government decisions. Women and men held full equality under the law, but were largely responsible for different jobs. Men waged war, ran the government, and oversaw the farms. Women managed the house, cooked, sewed, and cleaned.

Women could enter into contracts and own, inherit, and pass on their property, including land. Many women worked outside their homes—often in shops making fabric or baking, or on farms planting or harvesting crops. They could also be charged and prosecuted for crimes in the same way that men could.

WORK

Almost all Egyptians engaged in some form of work, from pharaohs and noblemen to craftsmen and soldiers. Egyptians did not work for money, until the Ptolemies introduced that practice in the later days of the empire. Instead, they worked for goods and food. Families made most of their own essential items. If a person needed an item that could not be made at home, he traded, or bartered, something he owned for the goods he desired.

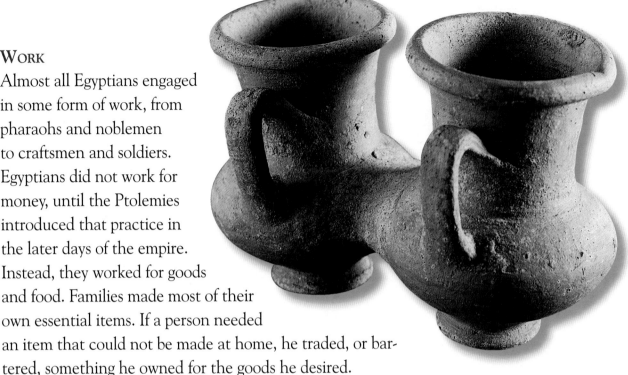

Ancient Egyptian families usually made their own cooking and storage devices.

FARMERS

Farmers were essential to maintaining a high standard of living in ancient Egypt. Once the waters of the Nile had receded from a farmer's land, he plowed the moist ground. Teams of cattle or teams of men pulled the plows. One person guided the team in a straight line. After the ditches were dug, the farmer or an assistant, often his son, broke up the large clumps of soil with a tool similar to a hoe. Women often planted the seeds, scattering them by hand from a grass basket. Sheep or goats were then led over the land to drive the seeds deep into the soil with their hooves.

To ensure a good harvest, farmers maintained their irrigation canals and water basins, which directed water to the seeds. Neighboring farmers worked cooperatively to keep a sufficient supply of water in them. They trekked to the Nile, where they

*Government officials
kept track of how
much of each crop was
harvested each year.*

pulled up bucketfuls of water and walked them up the banks of the river, using a yoke to carry two buckets at a time. They poured the water into the irrigation systems used by nearby farms.

When the crops came in, government authorities appeared on each farm to measure the field and set the tax rate. Harvesting the crops was a family affair. Some family members cut the grain with a short sickle, some tied the grain together, and others loaded the harvest onto donkeys to be taken off the field.

SCRIBES

Scribes made up the largest group of workers, second only to farmers. In a land where few people could read or write, scribes were highly respected and well-paid workers. Their unique skill allowed them to work anywhere. A competent scribe could work for the royalty, in a temple, or in the service of a wealthy nobleman. He could choose to work in a particular branch of the government or become an expert on matters of law or taxation. Ambitious scribes could train as architects and become respected builders of pyramids, temples, roads, and palaces. Almost all scribes were male.

Learning the trade was not an easy task. Students had to copy hieroglyphs endlessly until they were memorized. They did this on erasable limestone or wood boards until they were skilled enough

Reading and writing skills were highly valued in Egyptian society.

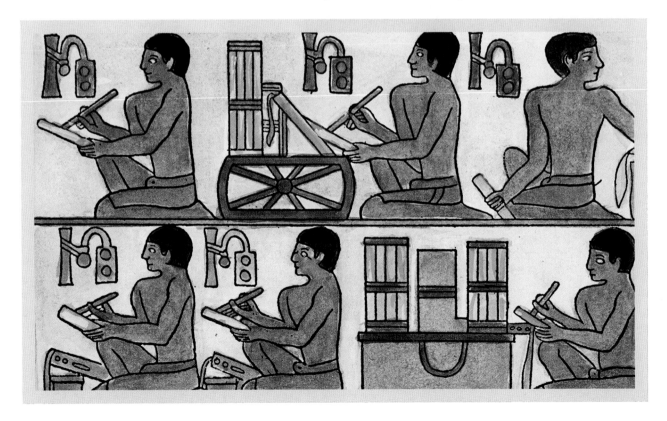

Egyptian artisans used a variety of tools to create and decorate useful items.

to copy onto more expensive papyrus. To master the Egyptian language, they had to learn around 250 different symbols.

Once he successfully completed his studies, a student could wear the traditional garb of a scribe: a long skirt, rather than the short one usually worn in other trades. A scribe carried a rectangular, foot-long wooden box that held writing implements and containers to mix inks. Black ink was used for the main portions of the text, and red was used for headings or important phrases.

CRAFTSMEN

Although they created many of the world's most enduring works of art—pyramids, temples, statues, exquisite jewelry, and timeless wall paintings—Egyptian craftsmen were usually considered nothing more than common workers. These skilled artisans built, adorned, and memorialized ancient Egypt, but their lives were difficult. Working with only the most basic tools, they were required to produce fine objects of beauty and to meet the high expectations of their **patrons**—the pharaoh, noblemen, or high priests.

Craftsmen included sculptors, painters, jewelry makers, goldsmiths, furniture makers, ivory carvers, and many others. Unlike today's artists, they had very little freedom to choose what they created. Most craftsmen were unknown to the public. They were

patrons (PAY-truhnz) people who donate money to the creation of art or craft projects

not allowed to sign their names, even on their grandest, most public pieces of work.

Yet through the timeless works of these craftsmen, we get our most vivid picture of everyday life in ancient Egypt. The surviving tomb paintings, buildings, statues, and temple **reliefs** have unlocked the mysteries of a long-dead civilization: how the Egyptians worked and played, how they lived in their homes, how they worshipped their gods, and how they viewed the world they lived in.

FOOD AND DRINK

Bread was the staple food of all Egyptians, regardless of a person's social class or economic status. It was made from barley and wheat, which grew in the fertile flatlands along the Nile. Bread was baked

Temple paintings have taught us about elements of Egyptian religious practices.

reliefs (rih-LEEFS) sculptures in which forms extend only slightly from the background

65

Egyptian hunters built net traps near ponds and marshes where waterbirds were likely to gather.

in a variety of forms and sizes, including shapes of people, animals, and birds. Honey or anise, an herb that tastes like licorice, were often added to flavor the bread.

Beer was the favored beverage in Egyptian society. Also made from barley and wheat, beer contained nutrients and was safer to drink than the water the Egyptians stored.

The lower class depended on fish and wild fowl for protein. To preserve fish, which spoiled quickly, people usually dried, salted, or pickled it in a brine. Fish were generally roasted, broiled, or stuffed with bread and spices. Upper-class Egyptians hunted fowl for sport. They consumed ducks, geese, and pigeons, which they trapped with nets.

Vegetables were an important part of the Egyptian diet. Onions, lettuce, leeks, fava beans, chickpeas, and lentils were among the most common vegetables eaten by ancient Egyptians. Sweet fruits such as grapes, melons, dates, and figs held a central place in the Egyptian diet. Grapes were made into sun-dried raisins and another favorite Egyptian beverage, wine.

The average Egyptian family did not eat meat regularly because they could not afford it. When they did eat meat, it was usually pig. The upper class, however, frequently ate meat. Tomb artwork often depicts various species of cattle, including pictures of the butchering practice and cow sacrifices. The rich also ate goats, sheep, and pigs.

Regardless of class, most Egyptians finished off a meal with something sweet, usually honey. Egyptians were the first people to raise bees for their honey. Once the process was perfected, it was relatively easy and inexpensive to harvest the man-made hives. Fruits and fruit juices also provided sweetness, eaten either in their natural forms or in sweet pastries and cakes.

CLOTHING

Linen was the most popular fabric in ancient Egypt. It was cool and strong, and could be worn year-round in the hot Egyptian climate. Plain white linen was most common. For an extra-bright shine, it was put out in the intense desert sun to bleach. In the Eighteenth Dynasty, it became fashionable for wealthy Egyptians to color their linen with dyes.

On cold nights, woolen garments were worn to fend off the desert chill. The wealthy wore capes and wraps made of wool for such occasions, but wool was also used by lower-class people who could not afford more expensive linen. Leather—made from sheep, goat, gazelle, and cattle hide—was used to make protective clothing. Animal hide was also used to make reins for horses, sandals, belts, and bags.

From pharaoh to common laborer, Egyptian men wore simple kilts. Extending to just above the knee, the kilt was a rectangular piece of fabric tightly wrapped around the waist and knotted in front. Longer kilts that reached midcalf began appearing in the New Kingdom. Men engaged in the daily routines bare-chested, but on special occasions or chilly days, they also wore a short-sleeved top or a band across the chest, tied at the shoulders.

Women generally wore long, narrow dresses that began above the breasts and ran to the ankles. Many variations of pleated and draped garments were also worn. Queens and women of high royalty wore elaborately pleated outfits that consisted of a skirt, a dress, and a headdress.

Though the ancient Egyptians did not have the variety of clothing that we do today, popular styles still changed over time. Clothes that were fashionable during one dynasty could be out of date a few years later.

RECREATION

Hardworking farmworkers and unskilled laborers rarely had time to play. Royalty, the wealthy, and children were the only people with leisure time.

The upper class fished and hunted for pleasure, often in marshes and swamps along the Nile or in the delta. Hunting in the open spaces of the desert became a favorite pastime among the wealthy after the chariot was introduced in Egypt. In groups of three or four, Egyptians in chariots sped after their prey—often desert hares or gazelles—brandishing bows or spears. They also hunted deadlier prey, such as lions and leopards.

Hunting was not just a source of food and materials, but also an enjoyable recreation activity.

When their daily chores were completed, children spent many hours playing. Tomb paintings show children playing tug-of-war, leapfrog, and different types of ball games. Wrestling was another popular activity among men and boys. Egyptian children were taught to use spears and bows, often practicing with their fathers to sharpen their hunting abilities.

Egyptian children also enjoyed playing with dolls. Some dolls were stuffed with cloth, and figurine-type dolls were carved from wood or ivory. Many wooden dolls had movable arms and legs. Mechanical toys operated by string were also popular, often featuring movable animals or people at work.

The Egyptians used a wide variety of handmade weapons to hunt prey.

Board games were a popular way for both the poor and the wealthy to enjoy family time. Many examples of games have been found in excavated tombs. *Mehen* was a game in which the player moved his or her pieces from one square to another, picking up rewards or penalties along the way. Like many popular board games today, the goal was to reach the finish before your opponents did. Another type of game involved ivory or wooden wands, and was probably played much like today's game of pick-up sticks. Dating to predynastic times, *senet* is one of the world's oldest games. The game board is a grid of thirty squares, arranged in three rows of ten. The exact rules of the game are

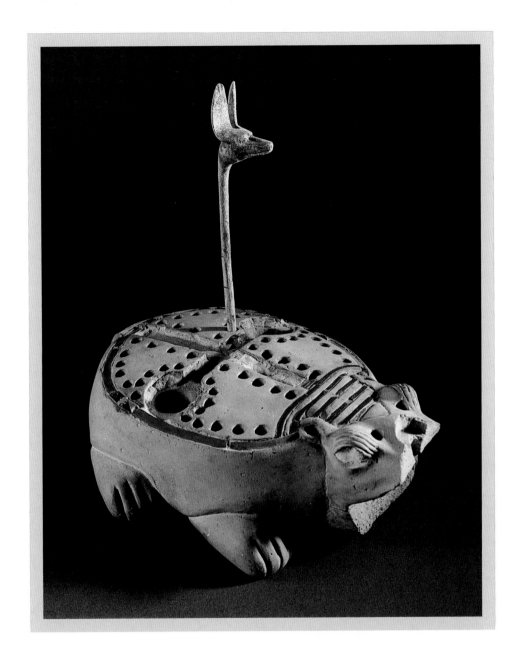

Many elaborate game boards have been found in the tombs of the pharaohs.

not known. Scholars do know that senet was not just a popular game, but also a symbol for life, with all its dangers and setbacks. An exquisite boxed set of senet with turquoise pawns was found in the tomb of Amenhotep III (reign ca. 1391–1353 BCE), an Eighteenth Dynasty king.

CHAPTER FIVE

THE CULTURE OF THE DESERT SANDS

R eligion affected every aspect of the ancient Egyptians' daily life. They believed in many gods and goddesses, dozens of deities that controlled all aspects of existence.

Horus was one of the most important gods in the ancient Egyptian religion.

To achieve what they wanted, Egyptians relied on the goodwill of their gods.

The belief in many gods is called **polytheism**. Without science to explain the natural world, Egyptians believed that everything that happened in their lives had a supernatural cause. At the height of their civilization, during the Eighteenth Dynasty, Egyptians worshipped almost two thousand gods. The gods were often portrayed in a physical form, as discovered in pictures and statues. Horus, the god of the sky and protector of the pharaoh, was shown as a man with the head of a falcon. Hathor, the goddess of motherhood, was a woman wearing a crown with two cow horns around a sun disk.

One god was believed to be more powerful than all others, controlling everything in the ancient Egyptians' world. This was Amun, the Hidden One. The worship of Amun began in the city of Thebes and its two temples, Luxor and Karnak, and gradually became important throughout the entire nation. Amun was believed to be the creator of the world. He was represented as a

Hathor was the goddess of love, fertility, women, and motherhood.

polytheism (POL-ee-thee-iz-uhm) belief in more than one god

human figure with a tall crown of ostrich feathers. He was symbolized by the goose and the ram.

The average Egyptian rarely took part in religious ceremonies. Priests were the only people allowed into temples and the only ones who could perform rituals. Inside each temple, priests kept a statue of the temple god in a closed shrine.

Amun was often painted blue to indicate that he was invisible.

MAJOR GODS AND GODDESSES OF ANCIENT EGYPT

Name	Depiction	Powers
Amun	Man with tall crown of ostrich plumes	The Hidden One, king of the gods
Anubis	Jackal	God of embalming (mummification)
Hapi	Man with breasts	God of the Nile flood
Isis	Woman with the hieroglyph meaning "throne" on her head	Goddess of magic
Ma'at	Woman with feather on her head	Goddess of divine order
Ptah	Man wrapped in sheathing with skullcap and staff	God of wisdom and writing
Sekhmet	Woman with head of lioness	Goddess of dangers to humans
Sobek	Crocodile	God of water dangers

LOOKING GOOD

As their incredible art and architecture prove, the ancient Egyptians placed a high value on creating objects of great beauty. This sensibility also applied to the ancient Egyptians' attitudes about personal grooming. Everyone from pharaohs to low-class workers paid attention to their hairstyles and took care of their skin. Many people wore wigs, and men kept their facial hair carefully trimmed. Many Egyptians made skin moisturizers from animal fat, and some even colored their hair with dye.

In their effort to make themselves beautiful, the ancient Egyptians often wore makeup. One of the most commonly used kinds of makeup in ancient Egypt was a type of eyeliner called kohl. It is made by combining a mineral called galena with soot, and many people around the world still use it today. In ancient Egypt, both men and women wore this eyeliner. They believed that it blocked harsh sunlight and kept insects away from their eyes. Many Egyptian women carried their makeup around with them wherever they went, just as people do today.

The sacred figurine was usually made of bronze and adorned with gold or silver. Every morning, the priests placed food in front of the statue and dressed it in fine white linen. It was believed the gods could listen to and answer prayers.

THE AFTERLIFE

Few societies have ever dealt with death as extensively and elaborately as the ancient Egyptians. The average Egyptian prepared for his death carefully. His desire was to continue his earthly life—with the same social status, family, and possessions—long after death.

The Egyptian Book of the Dead was an illustrated collection of about 200 magical spells, prayers, and rituals written on papyrus sheets and buried with a dead body. The material was intended to guide the deceased through his or her journey into the underworld and into the afterlife. It provided passwords and clues and revealed routes that would allow a person's spirit to answer questions and pass tests to ensure eternal life. There were many different versions of the book, which the Egyptians originally called the Book of Going Forth By Day.

According to the Book of the Dead, Egyptians believed that upon death, the soul left the body and embarked on a mystical journey through the pathways and corridors of the underworld. The soul's final destination was the land of the dead—behind the Hall of Judgment of Osiris, the protector of the dead. Along its journey, fierce snakes and demons threatened the soul. Doorkeepers to rooms and passageways would allow souls to pass only if they could answer the doorkeepers' questions.

Once at the Hall of Judgment, the soul had to pass two more tests to be admitted into the next world. First, the heart of the

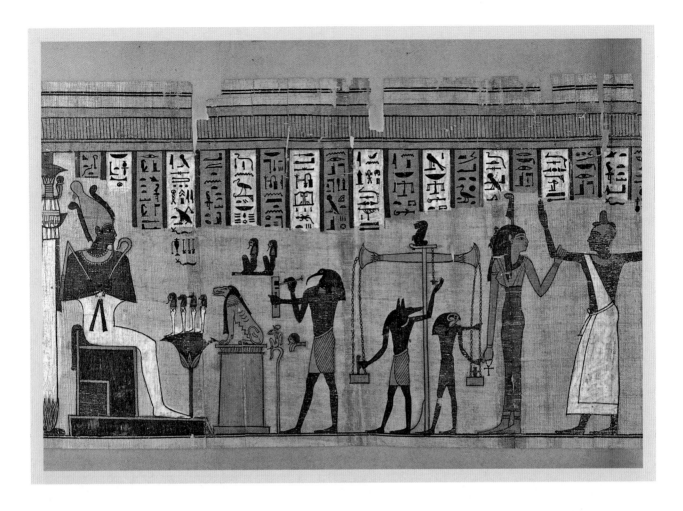

deceased was placed on one side of a balance scale. A feather was placed on the other side. This was done to test if the person had led an honest and truthful life. If the heart and feather were in balance, the deceased could become a blessed spirit, or *akh*. If the deceased failed the balance test, his heart was thrown to a hideous creature called the Swallowing Monster, who destroyed the person by eating the heart.

If the deceased passed the test, he would appear before forty-two gods in the Hall of the Double Truth. There, he would try to convince each god that he had never done anything wrong in life. If his skills of persuasion were sharp enough, he was ready to be

The weighing of the heart was an important test for the recently deceased.

welcomed to the afterlife by Osiris. At that time, he achieved godly status and power, while still keeping a human personality.

MUMMIES

Ancient Egyptian mummification techniques worked so well that many mummies have remained preserved to this day.

Preserving the corpse of the deceased was essential to a continuation of life after death. Egyptians believed that their spirits would inhabit their physical bodies in the afterlife. Therefore, it was important to keep the condition of the body as close to perfect as possible. At first, bodies were mummified simply by placing them

in shallow sandpits. The sun and sand dried out the bodies, creating natural mummies. Over time, the process of mummification evolved into an elaborate system of wrapping chemically prepared corpses in linen. Unable to afford this advanced technique, the poor continued burying their dead in the sand.

Artificial mummification began in predynastic times. Corpses were placed in reed or wooden coffins, which were then put in brick- or wood-lined tombs. The bodies were wrapped in linen bandages that had been soaked in **resin**, a sticky substance produced by some trees and plants. The resin slowed the decay of the body.

The process of mummification we are most familiar with was devised in the Fourth Dynasty. Using salt and natron, a naturally occurring substance found in lake beds in dry climates, Egyptians found the most effective way of preserving a human body. This process was used to chemically mummify bodies for the next three thousand years. The best descriptions of mummification that scholars have discovered date to the Eighteenth Dynasty.

According to the Greek historian Herodotus, writing in the fifth century CE, the process of mummification took roughly seventy days. First, the lungs, liver, intestines, and stomach were removed. These moist organs were taken out because they would cause the body to decompose, or rot. The organs were dried and wrapped separately and placed in vessels called canopic jars. The brain was pulled out through the nose with a thin hooklike tool. The brain was thrown out, because Egyptians believed it did not have a useful function, even in life. The heart was left in the body because it was believed to be the center of intelligence, emotion, and memory.

The inside of the corpse was packed with natron. The body was also completely covered in the substance. After forty days,

resin (REZ-in) a yellow or brown sticky substance that oozes from pine, balsam, and other trees and plants

the body was washed and the insides were packed with linen and resin. Then the entire corpse was wrapped in hundreds of yards of linen bandages. The person's facial features were restored by painting them on the wrappings, painting them on a layer of plaster, or by making a separate mask. The mummy was then ready to be placed in its tomb.

THE BURIAL TOMB

The tomb of the deceased was considered as important as the mummification of the body. It served as the person's final resting place as well as a home for his or her possessions. Tombs evolved from simple pit graves to monumental stone structures, filled with hundreds of items representing various aspects of the person's life.

Most tombs were built on the west bank of the Nile because the Egyptians believed a person entered the underworld in the west. Tombs were made of mud brick, limestone, or sandstone. They were either made as standing buildings or cut into the face of a rock cliff. Most tombs had two structures: one that the living could enter, and one that housed the mummified body. Relatives of the deceased entered the structure to leave food offerings. Over time, upper-class Egyptians built elaborate buildings with many rooms, wall paintings, and inscriptions that relatives could access.

King Djoser's Step Pyramid marked an important advance in pyramid designs.

The Bent Pyramid of King Sneferu has an interesting shape that sets it apart from other Egyptian pyramids.

The turning point in the development of the tomb came when Egyptians began to place the dead body in a mastaba. Inside, the body was placed in a pit in the ground and covered with sand. The personal belongings of the dead were placed in compartments in the mastaba.

With the construction of the Step Pyramid for King Djoser, tomb building entered a new phase. Wealthy, powerful pharaohs now began erecting enormous stone structures regularly as their final resting place. These pyramids became the architectural wonders of ancient Egyptian civilization.

PYRAMIDS

Most of Egypt's pyramids were built in a span of roughly nine hundred years, from the Third to the Twelfth Dynasties. Following Imhotep's groundbreaking design for Djoser's Step Pyramid in about 2600 BCE, pharaohs continued to experiment with the pyramid. Before constructing Egypt's first pyramid with straight sides, Fourth Dynasty king Sneferu attempted to build a pyramid that had sides that rose and then changed angles about halfway to the top. The unusual design caused cracks inside the burial chamber, and so the design had to be abandoned. Sneferu's Bent Pyramid still stands to this day, however.

Today, the pyramids at Giza draw visitors from around the world.

Not to be outdone, Sneferu's son, Khufu, and his grandson, Khafre, built two of the three remarkable pyramids that stand at Giza. Khafre's son, Menkaure, erected the third. The pyramids built at Giza began an architectural style that continued through-out the Old Kingdom: the pyramid complex. These sprawling settlements often contained as many as fourteen separate structures, each with its own function.

Attached to the pyramid that served as the pharaoh's tomb was a smaller satellite pyramid. This structure often contained the body of the king's wife or mother. A mortuary temple was built to serve as a house of worship for his followers, called the mortuary cult, who honored the pharaoh after his death. The pyramid city included housing for these followers. Also on the grounds were workshops that made bread and beer, tools, pottery, and statues. The workers who built the pyramid complex lived nearby.

Over the next two dynasties, pyramids were built smaller. Instead of an all-stone construction, rubble or mud brick was used for the inner portions of the structure. Regardless of how pyramids were built, however, they were often robbed by thieves. Once they discovered how to enter the pyramids, robbers tampered with the mummified bodies of the pharaohs and stole the valuable objects buried with them. By the Middle Kingdom, pharaohs had begun building extra chambers and corridors to confuse thieves, but even these proved useless against determined robbers.

The Egyptians needed a secret hiding place to protect the bodies of their kings. Beginning with King Thutmose I (reigned ca. 1493–1482 BCE) of the Eighteenth Dynasty, pharaohs were buried deep in solid rock on the west bank of the Nile at Thebes. This burial ground became known as the Valley of the Kings. Within the tomb of rock, builders constructed corridors, chambers, doors, and multiple series of rooms. The centerpiece of a pharaoh's final resting place was his enormous columned tomb. In the center of the room lay his **sarcophagus**, the massive limestone coffin that held his body.

The final room of the complex was called the treasury of the beautiful things. This chamber contained the worldly possessions of the deceased—his clothing, furniture, and jewelry—which he would use once again in the afterlife.

The rock walls of the tomb were covered with a layer of plaster painted white or yellow. Paintings of the deceased's journey through the underworld and scenes of the pharaoh with his family adorned the walls. The ceilings were often painted with pictures of the sun, moon, and stars.

In 1922, English archaeologist Howard Carter made a truly incredible find—the tomb of the Egyptian boy king, Tutankhamen. Amazingly, thieves had not looted the tomb, and its wealth of artifacts was still largely intact. Among the objects Carter found were three coffins. Each was set inside the other. The innermost coffin, containing Tutankhamen's mummy, was made of dazzling pure gold. Tutankhamen's face was adorned with a gold mask studded with valuable stones. The burial chambers were also filled with boxes of linen, chariots, life-size statues, musical instruments, bows and arrows, and dozens of other priceless artifacts.

TEMPLES

The houses of the gods were powerful forces in ancient Egyptian civilization. Temples were designed and constructed as exactingly as the pyramid-tombs of the pharaohs. The largest temples were mortuary temples built for the cult of the deceased pharaoh

sarcophagus (sahr-KOF-uh-guhs) a stone coffin, often adorned with sculpture and inscriptions

Tutankhamen's gold coffin is one of the most widely recognized Egyptian artifacts in the world.

85

pylons (PYE-lonz) the
monumental entrances
to a temple, consisting
of two tapering towers

and those dedicated to local or state deities. The earliest temples, dating to roughly 3000 BCE, were mud brick walls surrounding a tent or small, squared structure. Examples of these structures have been found at Abydos and Heliopolis.

In the New Kingdom, durable sandstone or limestone was used in temple building, resulting in much larger structures than had been built previously. Massive blocks of the stone were put in place, carved, and handsomely painted in rich, vibrant colors. The entranceways to temples were flanked by **pylons**, gateways consisting of two tapering towers. Flags and pennants were hung from the towers. Mortuary temples were adorned with enormous paintings that depicted the pharaoh and gods.

The Temple of Horus at Edfu is one of the best-preserved ancient Egyptian temples.

Pylons were often decorated with images of the gods a temple was dedicated to.

Located on the east bank of the Nile River at Thebes, the Temple of Karnak is the largest temple complex ever built by humans. The complex is mainly dedicated to the god Amun, the greatest of all Egyptian deities. The series of buildings, chapels, temples, and man-made sacred lakes was constructed by a succession of pharaohs over a period of roughly two thousand years—from the time of the Middle Kingdom through the rule of the Ptolemies. The site also features ten limestone pylons. The walls of the buildings and columns throughout the complex are covered with historical and religious texts, customs, and prayers, making Karnak one of the richest sources for our understanding of ancient Egyptian culture.

ANCIENT EGYPTIAN ART

Second only to architecture as ancient Egypt's main art form, sculpture began in predynastic times, probably as early as 4500 BCE. Early sculptures were carved from soft stone or molded clay. In the

The statue of King Djoser was carved from limestone and then painted.

Early Dynastic Period, figures of people and animals were carved in low relief, a technique that makes the images appear as if they are rising from the stone. The figures are created by chiseling away the background, leaving other parts raised.

In the Third Dynasty, well-crafted, complete figures of people appeared. A life-size limestone statue of Djoser sitting on his throne was made for his Step Pyramid. It is one of the earliest examples of outstanding Egyptian sculpture.

Sculpture flourished during the Fourth Dynasty, as likenesses of Egypt's rulers became commonly carved works of art. Standing at Giza is the larger-than-life statue of Khafre, carved in hard granite, as well as dozens of lifelike limestone heads. During this period, reliefs were commonly carved to decorate the tomb walls of the wealthy. Enormous statues, such as the Great Sphinx at Giza, appeared for the first time, indicating that Egyptian sculptors had truly mastered their art.

For years, scholars and adventurers have debated the mysteries of the Great Sphinx. Who built it? When was it built? Whose face is it modeled after? The enormous statue has a lion's body and the head of a king, adorned with a royal head cloth and false beard. It measures 241 feet (73 m) long, 20 feet (6 m) wide, and 66 feet (20 m) high, making it the world's largest man-made carving. The statue lies on the northeastern edge of the Giza Plateau opposite Khafre's pyramid. Most Egyptologists believe that Khafre ordered workers to carve the Great Sphinx out of a limestone outcrop, and that its head is based on his facial features. Some

scholars believe the function of the Sphinx was to guard the Giza Plateau. Others claim it may be a representation of the god Horus.

Pharaohs sought a new type of art to represent the expanding wealth and power of the nation. That form was the obelisk, one large piece of freestanding solid rock that towered to heights of 100 feet (30 m) and weighed up to 230 tons (208 metric tons). Obelisks were often gifts from the pharaohs to Egypt's temples. Hieroglyphs were carved into all fours sides of the obelisk, praising the pharaoh for his generous gift.

Bronze was used to make statues, often of Egyptian gods. Melted bronze was poured into a mold, allowed to cool, and then removed and decorated. By the Late Period, the cost of bronze had dropped far enough that almost anyone could afford it. This low cost and the ease of the molding technique allowed even the poorest Egyptians to buy bronze statues of their favorite gods.

CHAPTER SIX

EGYPT'S ENDURING LEGACY

W hen Cleopatra VII, the last of the Ptolemaic rulers, died in 30 BCE, Egypt became a province of the Roman Empire. For the next 670 years, the Romans ruled the

Cleopatra's death marked the beginning of a new era of Egyptian history.

Egyptians. Egypt's rich farmlands, bustling port of Alexandria, and proximity to the Middle East and Asia appealed to its new masters.

The Romans brought Upper Egypt under their control with a series of military victories against rebelling Egyptians. Having achieved internal stability, the new rulers then attempted to expand Egypt's boundaries by launching expeditions to conquer Arabia. Their early efforts failed, however. The Romans then turned toward improving Egypt's weakened economy by repairing the country's irrigation systems, which had fallen into disrepair in the later years of Ptolemaic rule. Agriculture once again thrived in Egypt.

Proper irrigation was integral to Egypt's agricultural success.

Egypt thrived under the reign of Emperor Nero.

From the reign of Roman emperor Nero (reigned 54–68 CE) onward, Egypt enjoyed roughly one hundred years of prosperity. In the second and third centuries, however, oppressive taxation resulted in numerous civilian revolts against Roman leaders. During this time, Christianity had spread to Egypt. Roman rulers persecuted its followers, but the religion continued to spread. In 313, Emperor Constantine ended the persecution of Christians throughout the Roman Empire with the Edict of Milan. Later in the century, Christianity was made the official religion of the Roman Empire. Not all Egyptians, however, accepted Christianity. As late as the fifth century, some Egyptians continued to worship their old gods.

MARKING THE DAYS

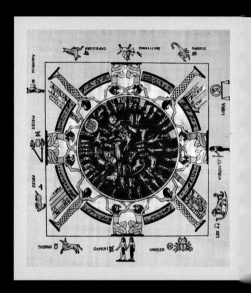

The Egyptians developed the solar calendar, an early form of the 12-month, 365-day calendar we use today. They divided their calendar into three periods, based on the country's agricultural activity. Each period was composed of 120 sunrises and sunsets, the equivalent of four months. In the first period, farmers prepared their land, and planted and harvested crops. In the second season, farmers completed their final harvests. The inundation came at the start of the third period. The first day of the flood was considered New Year's Day.

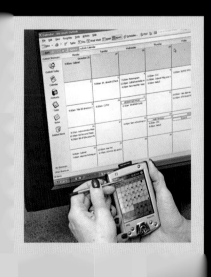

These seasons only added up to 360 days, leaving the calendar five days short of a full year. The Egyptians compensated for this by inserting five days of religious celebration in between the harvest season and the inundation.

This ancient calendar system was still not quite perfect, though. A true year is actually 365 and $\frac{1}{4}$ days long. Over many years, this eventually pushed the Egyptian calendar out of alignment with the actual seasons. The ancient Romans solved this problem in 30 BCE by inventing the concept of the leap year.

During their rule, the Romans introduced important changes in the administration and economy of Egypt. They strengthened Egypt's military power, organized more efficient methods of taxation, and improved the judicial system. The Romans also encouraged Egyptians to own land and open businesses in manufacturing and trade.

Roman emperor Constantine established the city of Constantinople, in the area that is present-day Turkey, as the new capital of the Roman Empire in the east. The Eastern Roman Empire was also called the Byzantine Empire. The Western Roman Empire still held Rome, Italy, as its capital. In 618, Egypt was invaded and occupied by the Persians. Four years later, Egypt was recaptured by the Byzantines. The fighting had drained Egyptian resources, however, leaving the Byzantine Empire vulnerable to new invaders.

Constantine I is also known as Constantine the Great.

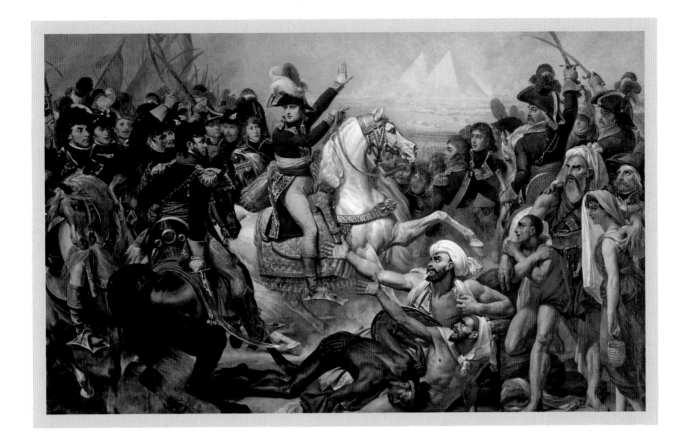

In 639, Arab armies crossed into Egypt from Palestine to spread Islam. The Arabs advanced into the Nile delta and captured Alexandria in 642. The Byzantines drove them out in 645, but the Arabs recaptured the city in 646, completing the Islamic conquest of Egypt. Their victory ended 975 years of Greek and Roman rule over Egypt.

Foreigners repeatedly invaded Egypt in the centuries that followed. The Arabs ruled Egypt for the next six hundred years, when the Mamluks, Muslim slave soldiers, took control in about 1250. In 1517, Ottoman Turks conquered the Mamluks, and Egypt was made a province of the Ottoman Empire. In 1798, French emperor Napoleon Bonaparte invaded Egypt, only to be driven out in 1801 by the combined forces of the Ottomans, Mamluks, and British.

Napoleon Bonaparte captured Cairo during the Battle of the Pyramids.

For the next four years, a power struggle raged between the Ottomans and Mamluks, as well as the Albanians, who were in the service of the Ottomans. Muhammad Ali, the commander of the Albanian armies, rose to power and established a dynasty that worked closely with the British. In 1882, discontented Egyptian army officers rebelled against British influence in Egypt. Britain, reacting to protect its sizable financial interests in the country, defeated the Egyptian army. Egypt became a colony of Great Britain.

In 1952, a military coup led by Egyptian army officers overthrew Egyptian king Farouk in an effort to end British occupation. The Egyptian Revolution of 1952 succeeded, and in June 1953, the Egyptian Republic declared its independence.

For the first time in more than twenty-two hundred years, Egypt was once more ruled by Egyptians.

EGYPT'S IMPACT ON WORLD CULTURE

Although many of Egypt's ancient traditions disappeared over time—its polytheistic religion, its system of writing, and the construction of monumental structures—much of the great civilization remains with us today.

The early Egyptian use of papyrus, dating back to the First Dynasty, was one of the first times humans wrote on paper. The invention allowed people to pass on knowledge and preserve it in ancient scrolls that exist to this day.

To build their monumental structures, the Egyptians mastered mathematics, geometry, and engineering. Many of their architectural breakthroughs, such as the column and the pillar, are still essential elements in architecture today. Egyptian medicinal techniques relying on scientific observation and healing were adapted

by other cultures. The Egyptians' development of mummification taught them about human anatomy and surgery, leading to important advances made by later civilizations.

Perhaps ancient Egypt's greatest contribution has been to inspire younger cultures to pursue their own course of development. From those ambitious peoples, seeking to improve and flourish, came the birth of Western civilization.

As Egyptologists continue their quest to explore the glories of ancient Egypt, we're sure to uncover more about the people, their society, and how their experiences continue to affect us today. We may never unlock all the secrets of ancient Egypt, but each new, thrilling discovery brings us closer to unraveling the mysteries of one of the ancient world's greatest civilizations.

Archaeologists continue to search for new artifacts and ruins that will teach us more about ancient Egypt.

BIOGRAPHIES

AKHENATEN (REIGNED CA. 1353–1336 BCE) changed religion in Egypt by rejecting polytheism. Creating the worship of a single deity—Aten, the supreme force of light—Akhenaten banned the worship of Amun and closed down many sacred temples. He built a new capital city, Akhetaten, in what became present-day Amarna.

ALEXANDER THE GREAT (356–323 BCE) conquered Egypt in 332 BCE, wresting control of it from the Persians. He founded a magnificent new capital, Alexandria, on the shores of the Mediterranean, establishing a link to the West.

CLEOPATRA VII (69–30 BCE) was the last ruler of the Ptolemaic dynasty. Her suicide ended Greek sovereignty and paved the way for Roman rule in Egypt.

DJOSER (REIGNED CA. 2691–2663 BCE) was a ruler during the Third Dynasty. He directed his royal architect, Imhotep, to construct the first of the pyramid burial structures, the Step Pyramid at Saqqara. The design featured six stacked mastabas of decreasing size and is the forerunner of the straight-sided pyramids of the Fourth Dynasty.

HATSHEPSUT (REIGNED CA. 1473–1458 BCE) was the first female ruler of Egypt. She undertook major building projects, including the Temple of Pakhet at Beni Hasan and a mortuary temple at Deir el-Bahari. She established major trade networks and organized a large trade expedition to Punt, in what became present-day Somalia, Africa.

IMHOTEP (CA. 2650–2600 BCE) served as the vizier and royal architect to the Old Kingdom's Third Dynasty ruler Djoser. Imhotep designed the Step Pyramid at Saqqara as a tomb for the king. At that time it was the largest all-stone building ever constructed. He was recognized in later times as the "father of medicine."

KHAFRE (REIGNED CA. 2558–2532 BCE) was the son of Khufu, the Fourth Dynasty ruler whose pyramid is the largest of the three at Giza. Khafre's pyramid is the second largest at Giza. He is credited with building the Great Sphinx, which is believed by some to bear his facial features.

KHUFU (REIGNED CA. 2589–2566 BCE) was the second pharaoh of the Fourth Dynasty. He was the builder of the Great Pyramid at Giza, the single largest building of the ancient world. Egyptian tradition often views him as a cruel tyrant, obsessed with finishing his pyramid, which he began constructing immediately after taking the throne.

MENES (?–?) was a pharaoh of the Early Dynastic Period. He is often credited with uniting Upper and Lower Egypt and as being the founder of the First Dynasty. He situated his new capital, Memphis, near the meeting point of the two kingdoms. Most scholars today believe that Menes was a mythical figure created by ancient Egyptian historians to simplify the tale of Egypt's founding.

RAMSES THE GREAT (CA. 1303–1213 BCE) was the third pharaoh of the Nineteenth Dynasty. Ramses the Great is often considered the most celebrated and powerful monarch of ancient Egypt. He oversaw Egypt's most ambitious construction projects, building temples, palaces, monuments, and a new capital city. His numerous military victories expanded Egyptian-held territories and secured its borders. He reigned from 1279 to 1213 BCE.

TUTANKHAMEN (CA. 1341–1323 BCE) is perhaps the most well-known ruler of the ancient world. His tomb at Thebes was discovered almost completely intact in 1922. He succeeded Smenkhkare, the briefly ruling successor of the pharaoh Akhenaten, when he was only eight years old. He reigned until his death at age eighteen.

TIMELINE

EARLY DYNASTIC PERIOD:
First and Second Dynasties. Upper and Lower Egypt are united under one king; Memphis is established as the capital.

| 5500–3200 BCE | 3200–2700 BCE | 2770–2200 BCE |

PREDYNASTIC PERIOD:
Agriculture develops in the Nile valley. Regional rulers govern large areas.

OLD KINGDOM: *Third to Sixth Dynasties. Djoser builds the Step Pyramid. Khufu constructs the largest pyramid at Giza as his tomb.*

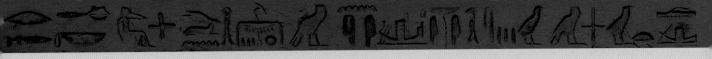

FIRST INTERMEDIATE PERIOD:
Seventh to mid-Eleventh Dynasties.
Famines, a breakdown of central
rule, and civil war plague Egypt.

SECOND INTERMEDIATE PERIOD:
Thirteenth to Seventeenth
Dynasties. Hyksos rule Egypt. The
horse and chariot are introduced.

| 2200–2050 BCE | 2050–1650 BCE | 1650–1550 BCE |

MIDDLE KINGDOM:
Second half of Eleventh,
Twelfth, and beginning
of Thirteenth Dynasties.
Pharaohs reassert their
rule, expanding Egyptian
territories into Nubia
and western Asia.

NEW KINGDOM: *Eighteenth to Twentieth Dynasties. Ahmose, first king of the Eighteenth Dynasty, drives out Hyksos rulers and reunifies Egypt. The first female pharaoh, Hatshepsut reigns ca. 1473–1458. Akhenaten introduces worship of a single deity, Aten, ca. 1350. Ramses II battles the Hittites to a stalemate at the Battle of Kadesh in 1275. Ramses III defeats the Sea Peoples ca. 1179.*

LATE AND PERSIAN PERIODS: *Twenty-Fifth to Thirtieth Dynasties. The Egyptians drive out the Assyrians ca. 653. Saite pharaohs of the Twenty-Sixth Dynasty introduce a short-lived period of prosperity and cultural reawakening. In 525, the Persians invade and conquer Egypt. Despite several successful revolts in the 400s, the Egyptians cannot overthrow Persian rule.*

1550–1070 BCE　　　　**1070–663 BCE**　　　　**663–332 BCE**

THIRD INTERMEDIATE PERIOD: *Twenty-First to Twenty-Fourth Dynasties. The nation splits into Upper and Lower Egypt. Nubia establishes itself as an independent state. Libya rules Egypt from the Twenty-Second to Twenty-Fourth Dynasties. Assyrians invade Egypt and drive out the Nubians in 670.*

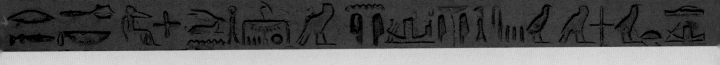

Egypt becomes a province of the Roman Empire following its defeat at the Battle of Actium in 31 BCE. Alexandria becomes an important center of world trade. Egypt remains under Roman control until the empire is divided in 395 CE.

332–30 BCE

30 BCE– 395 CE

PTOLEMAIC PERIOD. *Alexander the Great invades Egypt and defeats the Persians. Ptolemy I becomes king after Alexander's death. Egyptian rebellions and family rivalries within the Ptolemies undermine Greek rule. The Ptolemies rule Egypt until Cleopatra VII's death in 30 BCE.*

GLOSSARY

cataracts (KAT-uh-rakts) steep rapids in a river

chariot (CHAR-ee-uht) a small vehicle pulled by a horse, used in ancient times in battles or for racing

hieroglyphs (HYE-roh-glifs) ancient Egyptian writing system made up of pictures and symbols

ma'at (MAY-eht) the ancient Egyptian concept of justice, order, and goodness; Ma'at was the goddess who embodied those virtues

mastabas (MAS-ta-bas) Egyptian tombs that are rectangular in shape with sloped sides and a flat roof

mummify (MUH-mih-fye) to dry and preserve the body of a dead person or animal

nomes (NOHMZ) provinces, or districts, in ancient Egypt

oases (oh-AY-sees) places in a desert where there is water aboveground and plants grow

obelisk (OB-uh-lisk) tapering, four-sided shaft of stone, usually having a pointed top

papyrus (puh-PYE-ruhss) paper made from the stems of the papyrus plant, a tall water plant that grows in northern Africa

patrons (PAY-truhnz) people who donate money to the creation of art or craft projects

pharaoh (FAIR-oh) ancient Egyptian ruler

polytheism (POL-ee-thee-iz-uhm) belief in more than one god

pylons (PYE-lonz) the monumental entrances to a temple, consisting of two tapering towers

reliefs (rih-LEEFS) sculptures in which forms extend only slightly from the background

resin (REZ-in) a yellow or brown sticky substance that oozes from pine, balsam, and other trees and plants

sarcophagus (sahr-KOF-uh-guhs) a stone coffin, often adorned with sculpture and inscriptions

scribes (SKRIBZ) people who copy books, letters, contracts, and other documents by hand

silt (SILT) fine particles of soil carried by flowing water that settle to the bottom of a river or lake

tribute (TRIB-yoot) payment given as a sign of respect

vizier (vih-ZEER) an ancient Egyptian civil officer with important decision-making powers

wadis (WAH-deez) dry valleys in a desert region

FIND OUT MORE

BOOKS

Bunson, Margaret R. *Encyclopedia of Ancient Egypt*. New York: Facts on File, 2011.

Hunt, Norman Bancroft. *Living in Ancient Egypt*. New York: Chelsea House Publishers, 2009.

Kallen, Stuart A. *Ancient Egypt*. San Diego, CA: ReferencePoint Press, 2012.

Nardo, Don. *Ancient Egyptian Art and Architecture*. Farmington Hills, MI: Lucent Books, 2012.

Nardo, Don. *Mummies, Myth, and Magic: Religion in Ancient Egypt*. San Diego, CA: Lucent Books, 2005.

Ratnagar, Shereen. *The Timeline History of Ancient Egypt*. San Diego, CA: Thunder Bay Press, 2007.

Visit this Scholastic Web site for more information on Ancient Egypt:
www.factsfornow.scholastic.com
Enter the keywords **Ancient Egypt**

INDEX

Page numbers in *italics* indicate a photograph or map.

ABOUT THE AUTHOR

Nel Yomtov is an award-winning author and editor with a passion for writing nonfiction books for young people. Bitten by the reading "bug" at an early age, he learned how books could be the doorway to the wonders of our world and its people. Writing gives him an opportunity to investigate the subjects he loves best and to share his discoveries with young readers. In recent years, he has written books about history and geography as well as graphic-novel adaptations of classic mythology, sports biographies, and science.

Nel was born in New York City. After graduating college, he worked at Marvel Comics where he handled all phases of comic book production work. By the time he left seven years later, he was supervisor of the product development division of Marvel's licensing program. He has also written, edited, and colored hundreds of Marvel comic books.

Nel has served as editorial director of a children's nonfiction book publisher and also as publisher of the Hammond World Atlas book division. In between, he squeezed in a two-year stint as consultant to Major League Baseball, where he helped supervise an educational program for elementary and middle schools throughout the country.

Nel pulled together the research for this book from libraries in New York, newspapers, magazines, and Web sites.

Nel lives in the New York City area with his wife, Nancy, a teacher and writer, and son, Jess, a writer and radio broadcaster. Nel spends his leisure hours on the softball fields in New York City's Central Park and at neighborhood blues clubs playing harmonica with local bands.